A Technologist's Guide to Career Advancement

John R. Schneider

To my family.   A listing of names would only generate an argument.

CONTENTS

ACKNOWLEDGMENTS

I define a successful career as the compilation of the quality of people you have had the chance to work with. I have had the great fortune of working with some of the best. In particular, I would like to thank those that I worked with at Garst Seed Company, my first job fresh out of college. Though I have worked at some of the top technology companies in the world, that small team in Slater, Iowa remains the strongest and most influential in my career.

I could not have created this book without the teaching and patience of Mrs. Connolly, many years ago. It's amazing what an impact a great teacher can have on an individual.

I would like to especially thank the early reviewers of this book, including Samuel Frescoln, Dawn Schneider, Mason Schneider, and Betty Schneider. Your advice and thoughts were invaluable.

INTRODUCTION

By way of introduction and welcome to this book, I would like to give you a bit of background on myself. When I started out in the technology profession, I was probably a lot like you- kind of smart, or at least I thought of myself that way. I managed to complete a Bachelor of Science degree in Computer Science from Iowa State University and then took a job as a computer programmer writing "C" on OS2. At Iowa State, you can choose to take one class in your major on a pass/fail basis- I chose "Intro to C Programming" as that class. I can still remember what great pride I took when looking at the final class grades posted outside the professor's office- I had received the absolute lowest D- grade possible. I'm talking 59.50%! When the grade card showed up, all that was displayed next to the course name was the beautiful word "pass".

Now, it did kind of suck that I was going to earn a living for a while writing code in C, since I didn't actually know the language. But, it all turned out great, mostly due to the fact that my coworkers were truly top-of-the-line. And, I had the beginner's attitude of helpfulness and willingness to try (and fail) at anything. If you're further along in your career and you have forgotten what it's like to go forth and try new things, now is a great time to reflect on that.

Eventually, I worked my way up to Senior Developer and moved to a couple of different companies. I then went to night school and earned an MBA from Drake University, in Des Moines, Iowa. Getting an MBA was a lot more difficult back then, meaning now the programs are a lot more flexible. As you will soon read, you need to take advantage of things like that. The best thing about getting an MBA when you are a technology person is that you suddenly realize that all of those guys running the company you are working for really aren't that smart. There is no better feeling than knowing that you can do their jobs, but there is no way they could do yours. Very inspiring, that!

I then went through the late 90's and early 2000's and followed the money and the responsibility. I worked at startups and at really big, established companies. I took on roles including Vice President of Web Development at a very large bank, and Lead Technical Architect at the number one computer maker in the world. I then moved further up the management chain and ran a large department of technologists building commercial software in the automotive industry. Finally (for now), I became the Vice President of Software Development at one of the most respected and prestigious companies in the world. So, I learned some things.

As part of my work experience, I have had the opportunity to work on some of the highest transaction ecommerce systems in the world, and the largest database systems in existence. Through the years I have hired hundreds of technologists, interviewed thousands, and fired a few along the way. I went from lowly programmer from a small town Iowa to Vice President of a Fortune 100 Company, traveling wherever I wanted or needed. I made a lot of mistakes, but I learned even more.

This book is really meant to give you a framework to be a successful technologist. It is solely based on my experience, and I hope it provides you with a path to more money, a better title, and an overall better work life. So, quit screwing around reading the introduction, and get into the meat of the thing already.

1 COMMUNICATION

Yep, the first section of this book talks about communication. The reason it's first is because it is probably the thing that is most important to garnering a wage increase or promotion. You need to get better at it. Dive right in.

Email Communication

There are several aspects to effective communication that you must be aware of if you want to make a solid impression and enhance the view that others have of you. Possibly nothing is as important as your written communication through email to your peers, your manager, your customer, and your senior management team. Basically, you can come across as a Star, a Ho-Hum, or an Unhelpful Bastard that needs to go away. Here, we will focus on emails of the celestial type, and give examples of what not to do.

Know Your Audience

Who are you writing this email to? If it's to the guy you have worked with for 6 years and go to lunch with twice a week, that's one thing- misspell away and offend all you want. However, if it's to your manager, a senior manager, a wide distribution, or (God forbid) a customer, take the time to do it right. For our purposes here (your purpose, as you may recall, is to be generally thought of as ultra-competent, friendly, and the "best damn IT person I've ever had to deal with"), we shall focus on email communication to your manager and up.

> *Rule 1: Don't write a wall of text. In fact, don't even write a hedge of text.*

No one in management wants to read an email that contains more than 4 sentences. That's right, 4 sentences. I mean, those managers are too busy trying to figure out who their star employees are and how to explain why Project X is not only late, but likely delayed by 5 months, and then only if we buy those 3 new servers at $40k a pop.

"Okay", you say, but there is no way I can impart the information I need to in 4 sentences. There are all kinds of important details. Bull. It can always be done, especially with one nice little trick. Your last sentence- not a fifth sentence, mind you, will be "see the attached document that contains all the details". That's all there is to it. Concisely summarize the information you want management to understand, and then relegate all details, charts, graphs, etc., to a document that no one will ever open.

Example:

You receive this email:

> *Diego- what happened with CustomerX? They just called SeniorManager Dipthong and read him the riot act. I thought you solved his printing issue? I need all the details of what happened ASAP!*
>
> *Yours,*
>
> *MidLevelManager InCrisis*

Note the trickery- "he wants all the details". So, here is a bad response:

> *MidLevelManagerInCrisis- I did solve his printing issue. Our app was calling a Windows print routine and his spooler was throwing out errors indicating he had a corrupt driver. So, I remoted in to his machine, uninstalled the driver, and re-installed it fresh. I had him run a print job,*

and it worked. I think their corporate IT has a policy that daily pushes down a corrupt print driver. They need to get their IT person involved because he doesn't have admin access to his machine and someone needs to change their corporate policy settings. Etc., Etc., Etc.

Best,

Diego

That response actually seems pretty good to you, doesn't it? Admit it. That's what I would call a ho-hummer. Here's a much better response:

MidManagerInCrisis- I was able to solve his issue right away. I'll call him now and solve whatever issue he is currently facing. Really sorry he called Mr. Dipthong- I'll ask him to go through me first on any problems. Attached is a document that has all the details on how I helped him earlier.

Best,

Diego

I know that's the kind of email I would want to get if I'm the manager. And that is really the best way to think about the whole communication thing- if you're on the other side, what would you want to receive? Ask yourself that before you hit send, or better yet, before you start typing.

When Confusion Reigns

So, you've exchanged some email with the head of consulting (or some other usually dense person) and it's starting to get a bit heated because she just doesn't understand what you are trying to tell her. You have sent three intelligent emails to her (totaling 12 sentences and 3 attachments) and it should be wildly clear what you are saying. Now what? For some strange reason, you have a great desire and urge to keep up this email fight, and she seems to want that as well. Well, you have to stop.

Instead, pick up the phone and call her. What would be even better, if my suspicion is correct, is that she probably sits right down the hall from you and you could just walk over there. Do it. Leave the nastiness behind- get this person to be on your side, or at least get this person off your back in a friendly manner. Yes, I realize trying to explain any technology related thing to her is the equivalent of trying to explain a cell phone to a caveman. She grunts a couple of times and then continues jumping up and down. So, tame that caveman with friendliness (also try food), and then she will eventually and happily go away and find the next unwitting technical person to lash out at.

One other thing before we leave this topic: your email will be forwarded. Your email will be stored for long periods of time. You are leaving behind a record of your competence or incompetence in communication. Assume any email that you are writing will one day be in the hands of an attorney, an HR person, and the head of your department. Perhaps you should tone it down a bit.

Handling the Crisis

If you are in the technology field, then there is no doubt you have faced a crisis situation. If you are a support person, it could be something like the VP of Everything's email accidentally got deleted. If you're a project manager, perhaps it's the big project you're managing just got set back 8 months. For the developer or QA person, perhaps it's that big defect you dropped into production that wiped out customer data. Perhaps you're the DBA and the key database just crashed. Maybe you're the network guy that just bumped the datacenter cable that all internet access flows through. Whatever your position is, you have and will experience crisis moments. How you handle these moments will distinguish you from your peers. In a moment, I will relate an extraordinary example that happened to me, and take note, *all* of those items above have actually happened to me or the teams I have managed.

People rarely remember the details of a crisis, but they do remember how the people working on it responded. If you panic along with your less learned peers, you will fail to take advantage of a great opportunity to show your superiority. When being informed of a crisis, you should immediately float the following through your big head:

1. This is an opportunity to shine.
2. Initial information is almost always wrong.
3. Don't predict doom and gloom.

4. Show a real sense of urgency, yet be calm.
5. Don't start blaming, start solving.
6. If appropriate, make your desk the crisis recovery command center.
7. Communicate to interested parties often, even if you don't know anything new.

These are not ordered by importance. They are all important. A couple of these items need to be detailed a bit more. Let's start with number 5, "Don't start blaming, start solving". The first thing out of your mouth shouldn't be "Linda was supposed to run those test cases". Similarly, you shouldn't say, "I told Manager Jerkly we needed to get those systems backed up." People will eventually come to those conclusions during the ominous post-mortem (pre-firing), but right now you better be focused only on solving the issue. Be the hero, if you can. If you can't, be the hero's right-hand man.

To give an extreme, but all too real, example of what not to do, I shall relate to you one of my days as a developer and software architect at one of the largest computer makers in the world down in

Austin, Texas.   Executing software releases was always a major challenge at this place, because the systems were complex and the IT department structure was even more complex.   The project I was working on was a monster, with a ton of new functionality and a few supposed performance enhancements as well.

After months of development by about 20 programmers on multiple systems, we were ready to roll out our new, super money-making functionality. We had the appropriate people from each team of developers at the ready for any minor glitches that might appear.   It was going to be a great night, with celebrations and accolades for all the next day.   Little did we know that we were about to perform actions that would rewrite the release process, and add an entry into the employee handbook to boot.

Sure, we should have known there were going to be issues. There were some red flags, after all, flying high in a strong breeze, slapping people nicely in the face.   Probably the most telling thing was the release document. A release document is a file that contains all the instructions necessary to rollout new software. This document was created by a separate team, referred to as the Application Release Team (ART). No one liked that team, mainly because their function seemed not all that useful, and it was typically comprised of those who couldn't make it in development or QA. Basically, they gathered all the install instructions from each of the developers and merged them into one document. That document was then supposed to be used to execute a mock release in the QA environment, get the kinks worked out, and then on to the production rollout the next week.

The thing with a mock release, though, is that people know it's not real, so they don't pay attention to things like time constraints and how many times they had to ask the ART team to ask the development team for clarification and help. Plus, the mock release was executed by the QA team, not the same people who run the release in the production environment. Some real flaws there. What came out of the mock release in this case was a couple of minor changes to the release document. The release document was 216 pages, by the way.

Now, I think you are probably feeling the slap of a red flag cutting into your upper lip at this point. 216 pages! The project manager on this whole thing, we'll call him Brad, simply accepted the red flag induced lacerations as part of the process, and made nice little checkmarks in his project plan next to "Mock Release Complete", and "Release Document Updated".

So, Tuesday night was release night. A time slot of 1:00 a.m. to 3:00 a.m. was allocated, and all of us were gathered in a war room for the release (i.e., a conference room with some of those "think positive" signs on the wall). In the production environment, the release gets executed by the Systems team. This was a team well known to be very anti-social, and since they controlled the production environment, they liked to be thought of as demi-gods. In order to get anything done with that team, you did indeed have to make some sacrifices.

At approximately 1:04 a.m., I recall asking "Have they started rolling out the code?". Brad wasn't sure. Since I had made lots of previous sacrifices to the demi-gods, I strolled over to their lofty cubes and took the big chance of asking the guy I knew best. We will call him Perseus. Perseus looked at me and said, "Can you forward me the release document?" The flag took a chunk out of my eyebrow.

Now, we had two hours to do the release. However, there is a fairly well known axiom that says if a document is of a size that you can't actually read it in 2 hours, you also can't execute the instructions that it contains within 2 hours. I strolled calmly back to Brad and reported that, indeed, the release had not yet started and that Perseus may not be aware of the length of the release document and the effort involved. This would seem like an obvious time to say, "Abort now, live to release another week". Brad, however, decided to forge ahead. He didn't want a black mark on his record!

At about 4:50am, something had finally been rolled out to production. One developer, we'll call him Dobber, best described as a bit thick around the waste and the skull, decided that since his part had been executed, he was going to go eat some pancakes at an all-night place about 15 minutes away. Mind you, nothing had been actually tested to confirm things were good, and many pages of the release document had been skipped as they were on-the-fly deemed unnecessary. Since tensions were quite high already (we were losing many,

many customer orders while the release dragged on), Brad called Dobber and demanded he return immediately. Dobber, having just been plated with a tall stack, declined. Brad then lost his temper and swore quite profusely at Dobber over the phone. Dobber responded in kind and finally relented to coming back in, but with the new, urgent purpose of kicking Brad's ass.

So, there we were, at the headquarters of one of the great companies of America, at 5:45am on a Wednesday morning, sun beginning to rise, customers around the world being told their orders could not be completed, and a short but impressive shoving match taking place in the wide aisle of cubes.

"Go on, hit me!" Shove.

"No, you hit me!" Shove shove.

The red flag was no longer whipping us poor saps, instead, the flag pole itself was now deeply entrenched in our bowels. From our perch on the second floor, we could begin to see employees showing up for work. They were mostly mainframe guys, as one of the crazy little secrets of this company was that they sold hundreds of millions of computers and servers every year, yet ran their business on an old sturdy mainframe. That was the only day I can ever remember envying a mainframe developer.

We then rolled back. As you may know, the worst part of rolling back software is knowing you have to go through the same stuff all over again next week. Plus, no one had written down how to do a rollback...

The lesson here is pretty straight forward-don't panic and certainly don't get yourself into a situation that you will regret when things calm down.

Number two could easily be a law of physics. The first information you get is always wrong-usually really, really wrong. I'll give an example I'm all too familiar with. Part of the application I was responsible for while being employed at a large, world renowned company had a major search component. This component allowed users to run searches across the full-text of millions of documents, and do whatever they like with the resulting hits. For example, someone might execute a search like "Document contains 'John' and Document Size larger than 1 MB".

Well, at some point a customer noticed that not all the documents she thought she would hit on returned from the search she constructed. Upon investigation, we determined that yes, there did appear to be a defect where parts of the search string were truncated. Yikes! Upon slightly further investigation, it turned out this defect was introduced 9 months ago. Holy Yikes! Then, one of the clever people on the team did a quick calculation, and determined that approximately 146,000 searches had been run since the defect was introduced. Holy Shit Yikes!

Did I mention that this search functionality was used to figure out the relevant documents for major law suits? Did I mention that the users were attorneys? At this point, I did not have the handy list mentioned earlier. In fact, I derived that list mostly from this particular experience.

Of course, the number 146,000 was communicated all over the place. Both deep and broad panic ensued. Blame was being tossed around like a small cat in a hurricane. Nasty things were said. Senior management was informed and they huddled around a conference phone deliberating on who to fire first, who to fire last, and how much money we were going to lose. Several people ran for cover. Others began executing searches on monster.com. Resumes were being revised real time.

Fortunately, one of the developers decided to look a little further into the 146,000 count analysis and the details of the defect. The defect, as it turns out, only reared its ugly head for a very specific use case. When applying that use case to the 146,000 searches, the amount of searches that were affected dropped to my new friend, the number 7. Upon even further analysis, out of the 7 affected searches, 6 were run by our automated search checker that looks for performance issues. So, the only search actually affected was the one run by the user who reported the issue. It was fixed quickly, and the user was happy.

Now, there were some real losers in this crisis. Namely, those that accused others of misdeeds and those that said nasty things about the competence of Development and QA. These people had no way to regain their credibility, and now they were known for who they truly were- vindictive technologist haters who will throw their buddies under the bus at the earliest opportunity. The workplace was no longer their friend.

Another item I want to detail in the list is number 7- communicate early and often. As it turns out, you could have all available resources heads down working on a solution to any given crisis, and it won't matter at all if you are not keeping the right people informed about status. For truly critical issues, you should send out the status, or make sure someone is assigned to send it out, and update every 15-30 minutes. Part of that update should be, "The next update will be in 30 minutes". You gain two main advantages by doing this. First, if the problem is severe or causes serious issues, you will at least have someone saying, "Man that was bad, but we communicated it really well". The person saying that will likely be familiar with the afore mentioned list of 7 above. The second advantage is that you won't run into the issue of everyone acknowledging how quickly you fixed the problem, but everyone being pissed off because they didn't know what was going on and assumed the worst. In high-stress situations, it will be difficult to write these communications. You need to write the communications.

The Power of Two

Have you ever noticed that when you are in a meeting and you throw your opinion out there, having someone who outwardly agrees with that opinion gives you more confidence and credibility amongst the others around you? I refer to this as the "Power of Two", and it is indeed very powerful in a business setting. When two people "gang up" on an idea or path of action, it suddenly becomes significantly more likely that others will go along with it. The "Power of Two" is something you should try to establish, as it will drive your credibility up significantly as well as allow you to exert some needed influence on key decisions.

The easiest way to establish a solid "Power of Two" partner is really just to let it happen naturally. You may find yourself agreeing fairly consistently with someone on your team or in another position you have to interact with. You probably don't realize it, but this person is your business ally, and you need to acknowledge that, at least to yourself. Then, when the opportunity arises, the best thing you can do to cement your joint allegiance is to agree with him/her publicly a couple of times. He or she will assuredly return the favor at the next opportunity, and away you will go with the recognition that you are a leader and have great ideas.

You do have to use this new found power wisely, though. Your ally has to be someone that is already pretty well respected, otherwise you will end up with the opposite of the desired effect. You also must show a high level of integrity here, as you don't want to just be agreeing with someone publicly, and then talking negative about them or their idea when they are not around. That type of activity will catch up to you very quickly.

If there isn't an obvious person you can establish a "Power of Two" relationship with, there are alternate means to achieve your goal of peer and management respect. One way to do this is to work out a deal before an actual meeting takes place. So, let's say you have a big decision to make about how to handle a task, and it's your decision, but you know a lot of people will express their opinion about it. You should talk with those people individually first, especially that one person who will have the strongest opinion. During that discussion, come to a conclusion about what their position is on the topic and try to agree on the direction. Then, when the meeting comes up and you describe your plan, that person may very well speak up on your behalf! You just managed to create a temporary "Power of Two" ally.

This leads me to another major point. Really, for all important or controversial decisions, you should never wait until "the meeting" to find out where others stand on it. You should hash out your differences before the meeting, and at least completely understand what the opposition believes. You can do it via email, phone, or in person. The main thing is you don't want to end up surprised in front of your boss and cornered into arguing your solution. If you end up arguing your side publicly, you may be viewed as a non-team player, or even worse, you may make an enemy out of someone you don't need as an enemy.

As a technologist, you know that there are many, many different paths to solve technical problems. Almost all the paths have plusses and minuses, and pretty much every one of them can go really bad. As such, you need to have allies helping you along to prevent you from going down the bad path, or to help you out of it when it happens. You need to be that ally for others as well. What you don't need is someone purposely steering things in the wrong direction because your opinion won out over theirs in front of a group of people.

2 BETTERING YOURSELF

The Million Dollar Project

One thing that really irks business people and technical management is the constant million dollar project. Every time you or your team is asked to do something, it always comes back as a large, complex project that will take 3 years and $1,000,000+. This gets old, quick. Real quick. "But it is what it is", you say. Bullshit. You are losing all kinds of credibility every time you say a project is huge, even if it is. You need to deliver that message in a different way. Perhaps in a way that might even result in the project taking off, but in a more practical fashion. You need to quit being the stop sign, and turn into the green light guy.

Step one is to not just dismiss a project when you hear a two sentence summary of it. If it sounds large (don't they all), you should not say it's impossible or "massive", but instead try this: ask for the detailed requirements. Say that the project sounds very interesting and is clearly a high priority for the business, so ask to have someone actually write the requirements. A couple of different things could happen.

First, as the people are writing the requirements, they might just realize that this project is massive. If that's the case, then, you don't have to be alone delivering the bad news. Second, maybe once you see the requirements, and the project is huge, you could recommend a step-wise approach that will move the project along and deliver value at different stages. That would be pretty sweet, not to mention these projects are what keep you employed. A final thing that might come about using this approach is that you are able to give a more detailed estimate of the work involved. When you do that, it creates real credibility for you. Instead of just dismissing the project as too big, you can show how it is big, and let others make the decision on whether to go forward with it or not. In any of these scenarios, you win!

Presentations: A Natural Enemy

At some point on your job, you are probably going to have to give a presentation. For a lot of technical people, that really sucks. It sucks for all the right reasons- you're uncomfortable speaking in a conference room full of people, you don't know what level of detail people need, and maybe you just don't know how to best get your information across. Don't worry, we can solve all of these issues without too much work or heavy heartburn. If you are thought of as a good presenter, it's absolutely going to help your career advancement goals. It's also a great way to shine up that list of accomplishments prior to the performance review.

Let's start with the most painful part of giving a presentation- the hell you go through just imagining it. You are not a great speaker in front of the multitudes, though you know your shit left and right. How do you get past this? My technique is to divide and conquer.

How many people, exactly, are you supposed to give this presentation to? For our purposes, let's say twelve people. That's a nice number to invoke ill feelings and visions of deep disturbance as you picture yourself in a conference room trying to utter the phrases you have so carefully crafted. Here's the trick, though. Instead of just scheduling a meeting with those twelve people, schedule three meetings with four people each! This technique has a lot of advantages.

First of all, you get the advantage of presenting to a much smaller group. Hell, you've had bathroom conversations with more people than that! Instead of it being a presentation, it becomes a conversation with a couple of coworkers. The first one you schedule should have the one or two people with whom you are the most familiar, and who you know will not be intimidating. This is sounding pretty good, right?

A second advantage is the wonderful repetition you are getting. By the fourth time you give this presentation, you're going to have it down and know exactly where the weak points are. You will, of course, adjust for those weak points. The other great thing about repetition is that the more you give presentations, the better you get at them, and the less nervous you get. Soon, you might just be volunteering to present on everything from "How to test this feature" to "How to create a clock from two potatoes and a wire". Trust me, you can do this if you just change the presentation to become a conversation.

Conversational Content

The content of your presentation is, of course, a very important thing. In order to turn this into a conversation, you need to present the content in a way that gets people asking questions and even talking amongst themselves. This is pretty simple to do, and you need to do it right up front so that you can start to feel comfortable right from the get-go.

So, as an example, I'm going to picture a presentation you need to do as some kind of slide show, though it could very easily be a demo, a document you are going over, or whatever. The thing you need to do on the first slide is to force a question or elicit some kind of response from at least one person in the audience. One way to do this is to simply ask a very easy question like, "Did you guys look over the info I sent out ahead of time?" Since your audience is small, they are going to feel more comfortable answering questions that you throw out. You can even call a specific person out, and say something like, "Denise, this will probably all be just review for you, so feel free to correct me where I screw up". Anything self-deprecating you say right off-the-bat will put people on your side- and let's face it, you need people on your side when you are doing something tough like giving a presentation. Each slide you have should give an obvious opportunity for people to ask easy questions of you (i.e., engage in a conversation). Nothing relaxes a person like answering easy questions.

Your level of content is also a key decider on how successful your presentation will be. There is a very good rule of thumb that you should always follow.

Always present information one level higher than you can.

What? Why? Simple- because you want people to ask you that next level of detailed question, and you want to be able to answer those questions. If you present at the lowest level of detail that you know, then you are either going to be asked a question you don't know the answer to, or you are not going to be asked any questions at all! Both of those suck, so you need to avoid them.

This practical advice can be applied to any type of presentation. For example, let's say you have to present your new code for a code review.

Here's what you should present:

```
String Detail[1024];

Detail = GetPresentationDetail("High",
"Useful");

Display(Detail);

String GetPresentationDetail(String Level,
String TypeofInfo);

{

Return CallStoredProc(Level, TypeofInfo,
OutputDetail);

}
```

There's some of your new code. This is ripe for the asking of some obvious questions. I would ask things like, "What happens in the stored proc?", or "What's the timeout set to?", or "What happens if the database connection is down?" You know the answers to those, you just purposely didn't put the detail on this slide so that you could elicit the questions. People feel good about asking questions, and you get what you need, which is a conversation. You just need to anticipate, as much as possible, the questions that will be asked, and then perhaps your next slide will contain all those answers! The main point here is that you need to be able to go down into one more level of detail than what you have put in your presentation. This will generate questions to create the conversation, and they will be questions that you can answer.

Technical Architecture

I think we have already established that you are a technologist (if not, sorry, no refunds). As a person who wants to be ultra-successful in the technology field, you will need to get familiar with the technical architecture of the systems you work on, support, or otherwise interact with. Too often, technologists are very conversant with the piece of software they are working on, or the hardware they maintain, or the operating system they support, but they have zero idea of how things fit end to end. It seems quite obvious to me that this is critical information, but I am consistently amazed at the lack of knowledge in this area by most technology people. That's good news for you because it's really not that hard, and you are going to stand out nicely while all the other poor bastards continue to suffer from their narrow little view of things.

All right, so what exactly am I talking about here? Pretty simple- broaden your understanding. You need to know and understand the main components (software and hardware) of the systems that you have anything to do with. You need to understand how each component communicates with the other components. Finally, you need to be able to draw this out and explain it to others.

Nothing super fancy is needed here. You don't have to know or use advanced diagramming techniques, UML (is that dead yet?), or any kind of formal notation. Your goal is to understand how systems interact, how they communicate, and where they just might fail. This is going to sharpen your instincts when solving problems, and is also going to make you one of the go-to people when it's time for that big new project that touches all areas. If you're working for a company with more than 50 people, then you probably already know that every project touches all areas.

So, start drawing. Do it this way:

1. Always start with the user (internal or external). Draw a box for their computer, and the typical software they use to interact with your system (OS, browser, other software, etc.). This is your first component with its sub-components.

2. Take a typical and simple "transaction" and draw a line from the user's computer to the next component. Along the line, record the communication protocol. Record what the new component is called, and its major sub-components.

3. Continue the chain and any branching chains as far as you can for the transaction in 2.

4. Take all other major types of transactions and repeat the process, overlaying these on the same drawing.

Let's take an example and see how this works. We are all familiar with websites, right? If not, you're still not getting a refund, but I give you great credit for getting this far into the book. Below, I'm going to draw what is probably a fairly typical web site architecture, using the steps above.

We will start by drawing Bob's Computer, running Windows 7, IE9, and iTunes (included to show a failure point).

Bob then brings up Internet Explorer, and clicks on www.whateverwebsite.com, for which we fill in the http protocol and internet cloud.

Out of the cloud, Bob's transaction hits the whateverwebsite.com firewall, also with an http protocol.

The firewall then forwards the request to the webserver, running linux, apache and php.

To get all the information to display the webpage, the webserver collects information from various sources, including the database server running MySQL and linux, and the two ad related servers. Of course, it's also useful to know that the database server is connected to a storage area network. Check out the drawing on the next page.

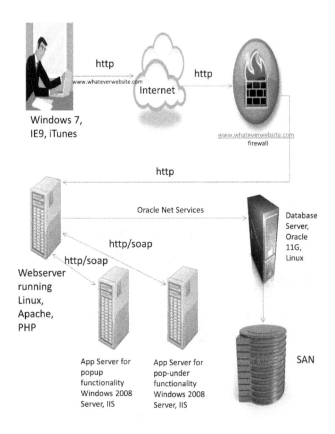

So, there you have the basics. Now, to be more effective and useful, you are going to need to add some stuff that you may not know. What version of MySQL is the database on? What does that firewall exactly do with the http requests? What other sub-components are missing? How many paths to the SAN are there? What language is the pop-under logic written in? You can collect this information over time and at each opportunity that presents itself. Note, all of this architecture information is for you and your ability to perform and impress. Get it down to the level that is most useful. Maybe you need or want to understand the database better, and you want to find out what logic is in stored procedures versus what is in PHP running on the application servers. Take it at least one level beyond your current knowledge, with two levels being even better.

When you are this knowledgeable about the overall system architecture, you are going to be able to have intelligent conversations with a whole host of other people, including "the business people". There is no technical position in the company where this type of information will not be of great aid to you. Whether you're in application support, development, QA, database development, project management, network management, or whatever, this level of information is going to help you do your job better. Recall, that's the goal- to stand out amongst the multitudes of mediocrity.

Getting Smarter

So, you have been plugging away at your position for a couple of years now. All kinds of things are keeping your company from giving you a promotion, a decent raise, or a decent bonus. Times are hard, there's a financial crisis, business is cyclical, you need to cut costs, etc. The truth is, even when times are decent, there are still a large amount of excuses to not give you a good raise. So, how do you combat this stuff? Get smarter.

One of the best things you can do for yourself, whether you like your job or not, is to constantly learn. It's usually not too hard to stay on top of the advances in the technology that you use every day, so that's a given. What you need to do is make like a tree and branch out. Read a book on stock options and how they work (that would put you in the less than half percent category of Americans that actually understand what a stock option is). Read the Wall Street Journal. Take an online class in chemistry. Tear apart your lawn mower and figure out how the engine works. We are now in the golden era of being able to get detailed information on anything we want at the click of a button. Take advantage of this!

Are you waiting for your employer to give you training on something? You idiot. Sure, it might happen, and take advantage of it when it does, but continuing your trek to stardom depends only on things you can control. You can control whether you sign up for a class, read a primer on embedded systems, or lay in front of the TV all night. Expecting your employer to take care of your future learning, and therefore your future success, is a ticket to mediocrity.

You should always have at least one side project. What is a side project? It's something that gives you satisfaction, forces you to learn, and gives you good feelings when work sucks. An example from my personal experience is that at some point, I decided I wanted to write a United States Patent. I added a bit of a twist, though; I didn't want to use a lawyer or spend any money other than filing fees. My thinking was that, at a minimum, I would learn a lot about the patent process, and be much more fluent in any discussion around technology and patents, which comes up quite a bit. So, even if I failed to get a patent, I would still be the "patent expert" around those whom I mingle with, or more importantly, around those who I want to mingle with in the future. Nothing allows you to speak as intelligently and confidently about something as when you actually try it. You then have real, first-hand knowledge while others have secondary knowledge from the headline they noticed on their Yahoo home page.

Here is another interesting idea- get an MBA. Not only does it pretty up your resume and make you more hirable, but it does something infinitely more valuable. It gives you the confidence and knowledge that the sales people, accounting people, marketing people, etc., that you have been afraid of all these years, really aren't that bright. In fact, they thrive on your lack of knowledge about what they do. That's what keeps them employed. The nicest part about all this is that it doesn't go both ways. What you will discover is that you could do most of those guy's jobs, but you know they couldn't do yours. They don't have the ability to become technical, but you do have the ability to become "business". That's power, my friend. Use it wisely.

Now, maybe you have thought of this idea before, but in tandem have also come up with a number of lame excuses for not following through on it. I thought so. Here, I shall now rid you of your uninformed pretexts.

MBA Excuses Debunked

Excuse 1: Can't pay for that.

First of all, you just pissed away money on this book, so I know you've got some money to blow. You clearly have a desire to better yourself, and you can make it happen. Lots of employers will pay a high portion of the cost, or take out a loan. This will be a significant achievement- it deserves to be paid for.

Excuse 2: I don't have the time

Yeah, right. This is everyone's excuse for about anything that requires some effort. You are going to be amazed at what a better job you do with your time management skills once you start taking classes. Some of those classes just might also add to your knowledge about how to do things way smarter than your currently doing them too.

Excuse 3: I majored in a technical field.

They will make me take 4 undergrad business courses before I can start the MBA courses.

That's excellent. First of all, you are going to learn some stuff in those undergrad courses. Second of all, you should be real happy there is a good barrier to entry- it will make your achievement all that much sweeter and your resume is going to stand out now!

Excuse 4: It's too hard.

Let me put it this way- you will kick ass in the classes that undergrad business majors think are hard, and you will be right on par with them in the other classes. Quit bitching and get moving on this.

3 PERCEPTION BY OTHERS

The Business People

In the information technology field, you will often hear the phrase "The Business People" or just simply "The Business". You will also hear variations such as, "That's a business decision", or "I will need to check with the business heads on that". I'm going to let you in on a big secret that I've hinted at already- the business people are not that smart. Indeed, you are probably smarter. Now, they do have access to information that you don't have access to, and at the end of the day, I suppose, they make the important decisions. So, to advance your career and improve your odds of getting a promotion, you need to become a "business" person, or you need to get really chummy with a couple of them. You might even want to get as far as being the person who does the checking with the business heads.

Depending on your personality, this isn't too horrific of a task. Getting friendly with the business people will, if done right, lead to you becoming business savvy as well. As always, start at the easiest entry point. Is there a business analyst you work with on projects? Someone who writes requirements or interfaces with the business? Maybe your boss is that person. Just ask to join them in the next meeting where you are at least slightly relevant. They really should want you there anyway- to learn and get more direct input from "The Business".

There are things you can't do in that type of meeting, though. First of all, your default should be to keep your mouth shut. When you see how wishy-washy these business types are, and how they don't have a clue on the level of effort for things they are proposing, this is not the place for you to correct them. You are on a learning mission. You are listening, and should only speak if spoken to. This is your chance to absorb the crazy lingo, and start to at least be able to make eye contact with these new friends. Over time, these guys might just get used to you, and see you as a person who can help them out. At a minimum, they are going to be like, "Wow, an IT guy that wants to learn the business on his own". That can only be good for your career, and it's also a nice item to plop on the performance review.

Changing One's Own Mind

You have now read and discovered some new techniques to further your career advancement. Only one problem- some of these things will require you to change not only what you do, but how you behave. You are, of course, a bit scared of changing your behavior because other people are going to notice that you are acting differently. That you are suddenly stepping up, and your communication is crisp and clean and very helpful. This worries you, and maybe even keeps you from taking some of these important steps. Get over it! That's the whole point. You are reinventing yourself not because your boss or your spouse or your buddies want you to change. You are reinventing yourself so that you can move up and make more dough. It's all about you, to hell with the rest.

The people around you are going to notice this change. If they don't, then you aren't doing enough. Some may not like it. In fact, some of these people may even discourage your positive changes by remarking publicly about them. Good! The fact is, that once you have even briefly established your "work personality" it's pretty hard to change it and act differently, but you have to do it. It's how you are going to get that promotion and raise. You will look back at each turning point in your career and realize that the main reason you became successful is that you were able to recognize and overcome your own deficiencies. You will laugh at how stupid it seems now that you struggled to change your nasty email behavior, which, in hindsight, was so clearly dumb and awful.

Now, one of the exercises that I like to do that helps keep me honest is the "New Boss" test. It goes like this: Ask yourself, truthfully, if you had someone competent come in from the outside and become your new boss, what would that person see? What would he want to change? What would be obvious to his fresh eye that's a problem? This is pretty simple in principle, but it really takes a lot of self-reflection.

The nice thing about doing this exercise is that it removes all the built up crap that you know about your boss, coworkers, customers, and systems. You will find that it's really quite amazing how you have funneled yourself into accepting lots of things that, with a fresh look, you don't need to actually accept. You will know you're doing this test correctly if you have that epiphany moment. When you suddenly realize that, wow, I do come across disgruntled when talking about System X. I need to change how I talk about System X, or I need to change System X. That's what the new guy would recommend, fresh off the street.

Formalize this exercise. Put it on your calendar every three months- "Talk to the new boss". Generate several ideas about what you need to change or do differently, and then act on as many of those ideas as you can. Then when that fateful day comes when you do get a new boss, it's only going to be a regular hassle, instead of a massive one. More importantly, you will have significantly improved yourself, your processes, and your potential. Again, this is all about your career advancement and making more bank, end of story.

Crunch Time

As a person deeply embedded in the technology world, you have no doubt experienced crunch time (if you haven't, you will). Crunch time is when you are down to the last days of a deadline of an initiative, and now you have to really get things done. This is not the time to stay hidden or take a vacation. It's a real opportunity to show how you are better than all of the rest.

The first thing you need to do is get creative and get motivated. You need to show that you are stepping up to the challenge and doing everything you can to make that deadline. Even if the crunch is a result of how you have been half-assing it the last 3 weeks. Your primary goal is to make sure your boss knows you are going above and beyond to make the deadline, and a secondary goal is to actually make the deadline.

One technique I have successfully used in the past is the self-imposed double shift. As a technologist, you may or may not have shifts. I did not, so the idea of a shift was pretty cool to me. Faced with a situation where the development deadline was one week away, and I had a lot more work than the time allowed, I came up with the double-shift idea. I came in at 7:30am, worked until 4:30pm. Then I went home for two hours, ate and rested, and then went back in at 6:30pm, usually until 10:00pm.

This really did help my productivity, and gave me a shot at making the deadline (secondary goal). Since my boss usually came in at around 8:30am and left at 6:30pm, the timing was tremendous. He always knew I was in before he got to work, score one. Score two occurred when I was coming up the steps and he was heading down them to go home at 6:30 in the afternoon. The first time this happened, he said, "Aren't you going the wrong way?", and I was able to reply, "Nope, just starting my second shift". Primary goal achieved. Make the most of your crunch time opportunities.

Get a reputation

You have a general idea of what you think about everyone you interact with in the workplace. For example, there is Bob, the support guy, who is condescending and unhelpful, but he's your only option when Windows bluescreens on you. There is also Steve, the QA guy, who is so friendly you can ask him to do anything for you, but he is totally lacking in the skills necessary for his job. Finally, don't forget Martha, the project manager, who immediately reports people to her superiors when they don't answer one of her annoying status emails.

Well, people have a general idea about you, too. You need to care about what that is because it's what will determine if you get laid off, promoted, a raise, and really whether you enjoy your work environment or not.

Here are some categories and their corresponding grading scale. Hint- go for the A's.

Personality:

A. Helpful, friendly

B. Helpful, shy

C. Not a jerk

D. Jerk

F. Thieving Jerk

Intelligence:

A. Proven smart

B. Seems really smart

C. Occasionally bright, not always

D. Idiotic

F. Government level

Competence:

> A. Dependable and always comes through. People come to you first.
>
> B. Solid- wish I had a few more like him.
>
> C. Comes through on projects he's interested in.
>
> D. Avoid assigning critical work to this guy.
>
> F. High-level government.

How to get A's

Volunteer for everything. This is especially important when no one is actually looking for volunteers. Let's say your company has a big software release next Friday night at 3:00am. Finally, after months of toil and trouble, version 1.2 is going to make it out the door to great fanfare (assuming QA didn't miss major critical defects like last time). Normally, as a developer, or support person, or whatever you are, you would not be subject to having to stay up and participate in the release and post-release testing. Volunteer for it! Say, "I can help with the post-release testing, plus I want to see how a release is conducted!". You are going to get a lot out of something like that- here are a few examples:

1. A whole set of people will now know you're the helpful type, even when not asked!
2. You really will learn something by participating in the release.
3. When performance review time comes along, man, will it be nice to actually have something real you can say that you did "above and beyond". That's instead of the crap you usually make up, which typically is just stuff that is really part of your job anyway.
4. You can be one of the important people who can talk about the release as someone that was working on it. You will be able to say "Man, that last release was tough- I can't believe we got it out." Or, "Ralph totally hosed the database update, but we were able to figure it out and repair it just before

customers started logging in." You get the picture.

Friendliness

Be friendly to everyone. Of course all people at your workplace are important. There are the obvious important people, such as your boss, other management, and your co-workers. However, it's also vital to be on a friendly basis with all the other grunts. Take the receptionist or administrative assistant, for example. You are going to need her at some point when stuff needs to get done, or at least to give you the answer to that daily late afternoon question of "Has the boss left yet?". I'm not saying you should make friends with people because they might someday be helpful to you. That's just a side benefit. There is an old unattributed quote that goes something like, "Be nice to everyone you meet, as we are all going through a great struggle." Ain't that the truth!

Another great strategy of befriendment is to "tackle the ass". TTA is a technique whereby you actually befriend the grumpiest, crumudeginist person in the office. This could be the aforementioned receptionist, or that mainframe guy that usually stops all projects from happening because they might require change to the code he wrote in the 50's. It might be a support guy or a systems guy that people fear for their condescending, snarky emails. If you can do this, the rewards can be amazing.

Take the mainframe guy, Bill- wouldn't it be cool if you were the first person that actually managed to get information from him on how stuff works in that ancient pagan world? You could go to the next meeting and say, "Oh, yeah, when that hits the mainframe, it first strips all leading zeros. That's why when we started creating accounts in v1.2 with leading zeros, we ended up with duplicate account numbers. It was probably missed in QA because we don't have a test environment that connects to the test mainframe environment. I'll work with Bill and get one set up." If you pull that off, not only will you be liked and respected, you will be legendary and indispensable.

Before we leave this topic, let us not forget about two important categories of people you should always befriend. Even if you hate them. Even if you don't have any respect for them. Even if they torture small turtles by turning them on their backs and running away. These two categories are the finance person and the HR person.

The finance guy is who ultimately approves your raise, your expense report, and your next big project. You need that jerk on your side. He/She carries a lot of weight at the top, and if you have them saying positive stuff about you and your projects, you are going to benefit in a serious way. You will also really need him/her when you screw up and Project Wonderful suddenly overruns cost by $200,000. The finance person is going to be the only person that can explain that away for you.

The HR person is also ultra-important. For similar reasons as the finance person, except more so. She (seriously, how many "he" HR people are there?) is going to have an impact on your employment that far outweighs any knowledge she actually has. She will be speaking to your management about you, whether she even knows who you are or not. If you are in management, your boss is always going to ask you if you ran x, y, or z by HR. Perhaps, most importantly, when you get into that jam with a coworker, manager, or one of your direct reports, you are going to be so thankful HR is on your side (forget about the merits of the issue).

Of course, the best case scenario is that all of

these people are reasonable and you can like them naturally. The best case scenario never happens, so suck it up and start getting friendly with the Natives!

4 THE REVIEW

Performance Review

Ah, the annual performance review. You can smell the anguish in the air around that time. In the summer, it comes across like fetid sweat that has caked and been added to your coffee. In the winter, it takes on the scent of an impending ice storm, where the sleet is comprised of monkey urine mixed with various cat debris. That ill-defined process that insists on ranking employees against one another. And that's always what it comes down to; your manager is comparing you against the other people she manages. The director is then comparing his managers against one another, until finally there is some wretched list of employees ordered by rating, regardless of job function or importance to the company. Your only goal for the performance review is to end up in the top three percent of this list.

To do this, you will need to be viewed by all others as the over-achiever, the star, the slightly better than average. If you are in the middle of the list, like you probably are right now, you basically are just some random employee who won't get fired for incompetence, but might very well be laid off if necessary. In addition, your value might be noted, but your raise will not reflect it. "Times are tough right now for raises", is what you will hear. Times are always tough for raises.

So, how do you prepare for your review and how do you end up in that top 3%? Naturally, if you have followed the advice thus far of many of the items mentioned in this book, you might actually already be in that top 3%. You will have all kinds of data that proves you are good. You will be liked by all, which is invaluable to the review process since your boss's boss will be looking over this, as will that HR person. If your manager thinks his boss doesn't know you or doesn't particularly care for you, your manager will not put you in the top 3%. Oh, and by the way, managers hate giving reviews. It is dreaded and put off as long as possible. Remember that, because one of your jobs is to make your manager's life easier.

The first thing you have to do is not make the review an event. During the year, or at least the few months before the review, keep track, in an email to yourself, of a running list all of your accomplishments. The following would be a good QA person's list:

1/8 Finished testing project x on time!

1/31 Found a defect that no one else would have ever discovered- except the customer.

2/28 Volunteered for post release testing. Worked 4 extra hours in the middle of the night.

3/24 Wrote that document on how to test functionality Y and trained the rest of the team on it. Without being asked!

4/15 Finished testing project z on time!

5/3 Got a B+ in an online MBA class. Man, marketing is really simple.

6/10 Reviewed our defect tracking process and suggested changes that will shorten the time it takes to get fixes to production, while at the same time significantly reducing risk of adding more defects!

6/30 Finished testing project zzz on time!

You get the picture. Here is what the average

person's list will look like:

1/8 Finished testing project x on time.

4/15 Finished testing project z on time.

6/30 Finished testing project zzz on time.

That's pretty boring, and really average. You are going to shine compared to those lazy sloths just doing their jobs.

The next thing you need to do in preparation for the review is assume one or more criticisms will be leveled at you. Unless your manager is a complete coward, which could be the case, he/she will have thought up at least one thing you need to do better. Managers aren't all that clever, so the criticism will likely be leveled at you after many nice things are said. Yep, managers are trained real good in giving evaluations!

Here is my advice- take the criticism, especially if you think it will be the only negative thing said. Say something like, "You're right, I'm going to work on that."- even if it's not true or only slightly true. You need to crush your instinct to become defensive and prove them wrong. You will just come across looking like a person who can't take constructive feedback, even if it isn't all that constructive. If you listen and appear to accept the feedback, you will also receive the side-benefit of making your boss feel like they are a real manager. That's good for you!

Before concluding the review session, make sure you tell your boss you really like working for him/her. Use whatever words you are comfortable with. I personally like to hear things like "You are the best person I have ever worked for", or "I would have left a long time ago if it was not for you". If you can deliver one of those lines in earnest (i.e., it appears truthful), then you just made yourself an ally for life. Do it. It's especially effective right after you accept that criticism.

Now, here is another pre-review technique, though this is one is optional. During that 2-3 weeks right before the review is going to happen, start looking around a little bit for jobs that are out there that you might qualify for. It's pretty rare to have a review where you come out of it and don't feel at least a little downhearted. "I can't believe she thinks I don't write enough test cases...", etc. Looking around at open jobs will do one of two things for you. It will either make you confident that you could easily find something else if this review goes badly or you become hostile at the one percent raise. On the other hand, you might just notice that there is not much out there at this time, so you had better be super nice and put on a good face during the whole review process.

5 MOVING UP

Be The Lead

An important part of being successful in any technical role, no matter what your position, is to become "The Lead". The lead is best described as the person who others will go to when they need information or status on a particular item or project. It's an important designation, and will look good to your management and on your résumé. "I led project X from inception to completion" is way more impressive and meaningful than "I worked on project X". Being a lead doesn't mean you are suddenly managing people or doing anything significantly different than what you are currently doing- just that you collect and maintain a bit more information. There are two main ways to become the lead.

The first way to become the lead is when something comes up in a team meeting that you think your boss is going to assign to you anyway. Just say "I can take the lead on that". Not only did you just impress the hell out of everyone in that meeting, but your boss is really going to value having a person helping him with what is really his job. When I hear someone say that to me, I immediately feel very friendly towards that person because I know my burden just went down. I won't have to hunt around for a status, or make sure those guys in Operations actually get pulled in. You, my competent friend, just made my life easier. I will remember this and reward this come next performance review.

The other way to become a lead is implicitly. This is when the boss knows that you are the main guy on a given project, and goes to you for status, issues, timelines, etc. This is good- you are known as the key person on a project. The boss knows you will take care of things. However, it doesn't have quite the same impact as the other method. So, when the opportunity presents itself, execute the first method.

Now that you are the known lead on a project, what does that mean you have to do? Don't worry, not too much. If the project involves multiple people, just set up some time with them, formally or informally, to get status and find out how things are going. Compile that info, and keep it handy. While you are at it, why don't you send status information to your boss once a week as well? One of the great things that rarely happens when you are a manager is getting important information from people without having to pry it out of them. Just remember, when sending the status to your boss, follow the rules in the email communication chapter.

There are also a few things you don't want to do when you declare yourself the lead. Don't suddenly think you can boss people around and prioritize their work. Don't demand updates of status from your team members. Certainly don't start acting all jerk-like and call last second meetings at 6:00 pm. You need to be a facilitator. Follow up with someone if they had something due and it's not done, and find out why (and if you can help). Show people you are on their side- goodness knows you understand why Bob took three extra days to write that stored procedure. You aren't responsible for chastising Bob, just reporting on the overall progress, so don't chastise Bob.

Never, never communicate (email or verbally) to your boss and say a project is late because Bob couldn't figure out how to convert a string to a numeric value. Bob is going to find out what you said, and if you wrote it, it will be forwarded to him. Instead, just say Bob was delayed on his stored procedure task as it turned out to be more difficult than what he originally thought. Now your boss might go to Bob and say, "I understand we're a little behind, but I'm glad you got that complicated stored proc all figured out." You and Bob retain a good working relationship. If, on the other hand, you had told your boss that Bob screwed up this project because he dinked around on a simple stored proc, your boss will go to Bob and demand answers. Bob hates you. Bob will make sure you are as unhappy as he is.

This reminds me of a basic maxim you should always follow. No, it's not "do unto others…" It's "Assume everything you say about someone else will get back to them, and say stuff accordingly." In the world of email, assume every email you write will get forwarded. Yes, even if you say "don't forward this". People love to forward email. Saying bad stuff about co-workers, even though you are one hundred percent accurate, will always catch up with you, usually real quick-like. Saying good stuff about co-workers, on the other hand, will also catch up with you, though it will travel much slower. You need to resist the urge to put down others. If you have to, get a pet rock and let it in on all the negative thoughts you have towards others.

Promotions & Job Descriptions

You want to get promoted. Damn it, you deserve it. You've been in the same position for 3 years, and despite that mediocre review two years ago, you have been a pretty solid performer. But how does one go about it? Just ask? Well, you sure as hell aren't going to get a promotion without asking. That would be a rarity. In fact, that would be such an anomaly that if it does happen to you, I want you to send me an email and tell me what god or gods you worship. I will join you in your beliefs.

If you live by the idea that management will recognize your hard work and reward it with a promotion without you having to say anything, it's really time to wake up. Getting a promotion not only depends on the work you have done and the work you have in the pipeline, it also depends on you doing a little more work focused on "the justification", described below.

In order to get a promotion, your manager will be putting together "the justification" for it. He or she will have to write a detailed case of why you deserve the promotion, and what it will do for the business. This justification will then be sent along to a Director or a Vice President, who will then send it along to the ultimate decision maker. All along the way, you will need approval and acceptance. If your manager is only half-hearted about it, then it will be a lame case she puts together, which will get rejected at the next level. Then she can take the nice easy way out and tell you in your next one-on-one, "Sorry, I submitted the justification for your promotion, but it got rejected at the top because this just isn't the right time."

Avoiding this is easy. You need to write the justification, and you need to do it with all the audiences in mind that it will be forwarded to. That means you have to do it correctly, and you can't come across as an amateur or it won't make it past your boss. Let me guess, the first thing you would highlight in your justification is how long you have been in your current position. Amateur. The least important detail is how long you've been with the company. You are not entitled to a promotion because of your ability to stay employed- you get one because of the proven hard work you have put in and how the cost of replacing you if you left dramatically outweighs the cost of a promotion. The following is an example of what you should send to your manager in preparation for the promotional discussion. Assume everything will be slightly edited and sent on to the next level(s) for approval.

Hi Donna,

One thing I want to discuss with you today in our one-on-one is the possibility of receiving a promotion and what process I would need to follow to that end. I have attached the details of my recent activities and want to get your feedback on the likelihood of being promoted to a Senior Network Engineer.

Thanks,

Junior NetworkEngineer

Here is an example of what you should put in the attachment, each sentence numbered for discussion below:

[1] Over the last 3 years, I have completed a number of important projects, including x,y, and

John R. Schneider

z. [2] I always focus my time on what is best for the business, and execute on projects with little supervision. [3] About six months ago, I completely revised our process on how we draw up network topologies to be consistent across teams- saving the network engineering department many, many hours of re-work. [4] I recently received my CCNA certification, and I am currently working on the ITIL Foundation certification. [5] I took the lead on project J, and though it was a complex and risky project, I was able to deliver it on time and without any resulting production issues. [6] I also took over responsibility for System Y, and I have stabilized that environment to the point where we no longer violate our SLA's. [7] I have also been working directly with Customer P and have resolved their firewall issues. [8] Currently, I am working on projects A, B, C, and expect to meet all deadlines.

Ok, let's break this down and look at each sentence.

[1] You have identified how long you've been at the company and pointed out some projects

70

that you worked on that were completed reasonably well. This is a good introduction to your background, and it doesn't come across as a demand for a promotion because of your tenure with the company. Management is interested in projects x,y,z, but since these are completed, it's old news. Previous project success doesn't guarantee future project success, and certainly doesn't even come close to guaranteeing you a promotion. Previous project failures, though, can really put a damper on promotional likelihood.

[2] This is the "with little supervision" sentence. This is an interesting and important statement. It's a sentence that will not make it to the next level of management approval, but I it is important nonetheless. First of all, the "focus on the business" part is pretty generic, but it needs to be mentioned because this should always be the case. It's really just a lead-in for the second part of the sentence, "...with little supervision..." which is something your boss truly appreciates about you. It makes her stop and think how you are so much easier to manage than others on the team because she can give you a project, and then off you go getting it done. You don't cause problems or undue hardship for her. It makes her picture her work life

without you, and possibly replaced by someone that consumes many hours of her time. It's true, management spends 80% of their people time on poor performing employees. Of course, she doesn't want her boss to know that she doesn't have to manage you too much, so that sentence will be nicely removed when forwarding on the justification, but it has had its impact.

[3] Ah, the process improvement sentence! This is key because all job titles, especially the higher up you go, have some requirement about defining or changing processes. It really is an important attribute to have in order to be successful in moving up the technology chain. You have just proven you have that attribute.

[4] You are certified! Management always needs reasons to give you a promotion, and having just received some kind of certification or degree is a very nice reason. And since you did this on your own time, without company dollars or involvement, it looks even better. What's that? You're already working on the next certification! Wow, we better get this guy promoted so that he won't leave us for another company.

[5] This is all about your execution. All of

your hard work is paying off. You did take the lead on that project, and saved your manager a boatload of pain and grief. The fact that you were publicly known as the lead shows that you are already performing at the next level, hell, maybe even at the level above that! Can you imagine what would have happened to that project if you were not the lead? Your boss can.

[6] System Y. You took it over and stabilized it. Everyone hates System Y and avoids it like the camper who accidentally wiped himself with poison ivy and now avoids all three-leafed plants. If you don't get this promotion and leave the company, who the hell are they going to get to support System Y? Nice piece of work you did there to take that over- now it's time to reap the benefits.

[7] You have been working directly with a customer. They know you, you know them. You have solved their issues. They ask for you when they call. What if you weren't there? That customer just might be disappointed. "What happened to Jim? He was so great to work with!" Your boss doesn't want to answer that question, and also doesn't want to have to work with the customer herself. When the next two levels of

management see that customers ask for you, they will be impressed and will understand the importance you bring to the business.

[8] By describing the projects you currently have in your pipeline, the naïve management team that reads this is going to be thinking to themselves how they can't possibly let those projects slip. Perhaps if you were to not receive the promotion, you might look around at other opportunities, or you might not be quite so engaged on those projects. This is effective. This is very effective. You didn't have to threaten anything, anyone, or even insinuate anything, but there is a nice implied threat that management will understand.

Now that you see the intent behind each sentence, you can simply change things up to more appropriately match your situation. The idea is to get each one of those ideas across to your full audience, which is three levels of management and an HR person.

Job Descriptions

Very possibly, the job description for the position you want to be promoted to will be pulled out upon your promotion request.   Always remember, the real function of a job description is to give your manager an excuse to not give you a promotion. They are almost always poorly written, overly broad, and barely even useful for HR purposes. These documents are usually written by committee, updated every seventeen years and dusted off only when there is an HR issue. These job descriptions will be used against you. You need to avoid the job description trap.

For you, it's also a trap because it gives you an excuse to not do a particular work function you may not be fond of. "Sorry, I'm not a Senior Network Engineer; we'll have to give that work to Scott." I have heard that type of crap many times. You better not ever say anything like that. Your job is to be performing work that's already at the next level. It's a lot easier to promote someone who is already doing the next level work than it is to promote someone you think might be able to do the next level of work.

For your manager, the job description can be the excuse not to give you the promotion. "Sorry, but the Senior position requires you to ____". Most of that will be taken care of if you approach your promotion in the way described above. It's also handy to have looked over the job description for the position you want before constructing your reasoning. That's if it's readily available. If it's not, just go with the template above and you should be golden.

Moving Up by Moving Out

So, you have made the decision it's time to look elsewhere. Perhaps your company is struggling to make its numbers and you see the end approaching. Maybe your company has started to ship IT positions to India or China. Maybe you didn't obtain this book in time, and realize that you really screwed things up here, and you have no chance to establish a good name for yourself. Maybe you just got so pissed off after that last review that you are going to show them and get the hell out. Regardless, you have lots of options and a clear path to follow, which I will elucidate below.

Don't Quit Your Day Job

First things first. If you haven't been fired or laid off, then don't just quit your current job before you have found the next one. I know, trust me, it can be so tempting to say, "F Off, try and do this without me, 'cause I'm gone!". I certainly have wanted to do that in the past, but it isn't a smart decision for you, which is what this is all about. What is best for you? The best thing for you is to start looking around while continuing to receive timely paychecks from your current employer. Even if you hate being at that place. Even if you can't stand your boss and that gossipy bleep sitting beside you. Even if you're working on the dumbest damn project ever thought up, and you know it's going to end in failure.

What you need to do is to give yourself a bit of a break. You have made the decision that you are going to leave, so take some pressure off yourself. Don't demand excellence (i.e. stress) from every task you complete. Do a good job, but don't be concerned about doing things the best. You still need to be punctual and attend all meetings and get your basic work done, but don't go above and beyond anymore. It can be pretty liberating to let that email from the idiot consulting lady just idle in your inbox for a day or so , instead of executing on your typical less than thirty minute response. Accept a few things you would have argued about in the past.

Now, don't get crazy. Job seeking can take a while. Don't start skipping work or taking a siesta at your desk. Even when you "think" you are going to get an offer, that's not the right time to start telling people off. Plus, then you might miss out on the opportunity to get a counter offer, which I will cover in just a bit. Basically, perform at the level of your colleagues who haven't read this book.

The Search

One of the benefits of being a technologist is you are not tied to a specific job industry. You can bounce around from banking to automotive to computer hardware to legal. You're not stuck in an obscure industry like home furnishings, where everyone knows everyone, so good luck getting hired. When looking for a position, you need to be very broad in your search. If you're willing to move cities or states, then you are really not going to have a problem finding a job, and a step up at that. You should be blasting your résumé to every job board for which you even remotely might be qualified.

The best technique for applying to positions listed on job boards is to allocate 30 minutes every morning to apply for as many jobs as possible in that time. Do it early in the morning, as you would be surprised at what matters for determining if you are going to get an interview or not. One of the most common things that matters is how quickly you respond to the ad! If you wait until midday to apply, or, Zeus forbid, the next day, you just shot your resume into a black hole- even if you are perfect for the job. Hundreds of people are ahead of you in the resume stack, and the person looking at those resumes won't make it past the first thirty.

You also need to get your résumé written by a professional. Pay a couple hundred bucks and get it done. Do it! If it comes back and they have missed the mark a bit, I bet they have at least improved your resume by three-fold. You might think you know what you're doing on your resume, but you don't. Always keep it as simple as possible and easily readable. You need professional help here. Pony up the money and reap the rewards. It's a bit like when you have to pay a doctor for something. You are angry about the unexpected expense, but take a step back and look at thing for a second. What the hell is more important than your health? You should be shoveling money every month to health related items instead of throwing it to McDonalds and Pay-Per-View. The same is true for your resume- get it done by a professional; it will reward you for many years to come.

Now, let's see, it's 7:22 am and you found a job listing on a job board that has been freshly posted. It's at a good-sized company, and man are you a fit! You eagerly click "Apply", and damn it all to hell it takes you to the company's idiotic HR system where you are going to have to input your entire life. You can't even cut and paste stuff. You're thinking, "Man, I don't have the time or the desire to enter all this stuff, let's see what the next job is." Nope, bad thinking. You need to turn your usual solid logic around and see that 19 page form as a barrier for all the other job seekers looking to apply. You should smile happily when you see that HR website popup asking obscure questions about your arrest record. Many, many people are turned off by having to input that information. Not you. I'll say it again, not you.

Interviewing

I have held hundreds of interviews for technology positions. This includes everything from software developers, QA positions, DBA's, technical support, and all the way to directors and mid-level managers. I've made hiring mistakes, and they are costly. Over the years, I have completely refined my process based upon success and failure, and I'm going to share that with you so you can be properly prepared for your interviews. Certainly, not all technology managers interview the way I do, but if you can master my interview, you should easily get through whatever the other jerks are throwing at you.

Above all, you are going to need to be competent at the things you say you are competent at. If you say you are a PHP expert on your resume, I'm going to find out if that's true. If you say "Excels at invoking process change", I'm going to be asking you the details about that. And you better have details. If you can't answer questions about technologies or other items on your resume that you say you know, then I'm not going to believe anything else you have to say. Be able to prove you're good at the things you say you're good at.

I'm going to start by asking you high-level questions, and then start delving into detail. I might ask "What was the most complex project you have worked on, and what made it complex?" Then when you tell me it was implementing the billing software because you had to understand all the accounting rules, I'm going to ask you for the three most complex accounting rules you had to implement. Then I'm going to ask you what language you wrote them in, and how many unit test cases did you write for each accounting rule. Yeah, that sounds pretty jerkish, but don't worry, I'm going to ask you all that stuff in a kind manner and accept your answer, no matter what it is. The best way to answer these types of questions is to come in prepared. You should pick out two projects you have worked on (preferably as the lead), and re-memorize all the gory details of how they went. The good and the bad, because I will need to know about the bad, too.

When I ask you a question about something you have worked on, don't say "*We* ran this by the customer right after the requirements were written." Don't say, "*We* developed this in three weeks", or "*We* wrote three hundred test cases". I don't care about what the "we" accomplished, I'm only interviewing *you*, not the team you worked on.

I want to know how you ran the requirements by the customer and how you developed the software quickly and how you wrote 100 test cases. When you say "we", I always assume someone else did the bulk of the work, or the most complicated part of it. Next candidate, please.

Always remember in an interview that your objective is to get an offer. That's it. Bite your tongue at stupid questions, because you will be asked some, guaranteed. Don't talk salary if you can at all avoid it. You want them to really want you, and then you will be amazed at what they can do about your salary requirements. If you give up your salary desires early on, you might very well be weeded out early on. That would be a shame since they didn't even get the opportunity to see what an ultra-competent person you are.

In addition, yes, you should also do all those things that all the interview pundits say you should do. Know as much about the company as possible going into the interview, etc. I put much less of a weight on items like that, and much more on your overall competence at the type of work I'm hiring for. When you come on board, you will quickly find out we have x amount of employees and are a leader in our industry. Other interviewers, though, will definitely ask you what you know about the company (lame though I find that), so you had better have some information.

In the realm of things not to do in an interview, you should express high interest, but not crazy interest. "I'm really excited about this position and really want to work for your company" does not impress me. Of course you are excited, and of course you want to work for this company. Otherwise you wouldn't be here. You definitely need to express some real interest in the position and make sure the hiring manager knows it, but keep it reasonable.

I'm also going to ask you about where you are in your job hunt. Your answer should be that you are interviewing next week at Company B for a similar position. This will say a couple of things. First, it will say that you are also desired by other companies out there. That makes the interviewer feel more comfortable. Second, it will say that they had better not screw around deciding whether to make you an offer or not, as they might just miss out. It does this in a reasonable fashion, without putting too much pressure on the interviewer or on the company's lengthy hiring process.

Now, if you told the interviewer that you already had an offer in hand from Company B, then they just might decide that they don't want to compete with that, and move on. Finally, disclosing to an interviewer that you are talking with multiple companies gives you a good reason to follow up. If you haven't heard anything by the next week, you can send an email and inquire what the status is, as you have other opportunities you are considering. They might just believe you because you did mention something about that in the interview.

At the end of the interview, you should also ask a couple of questions. Everyone out there says you should, but many candidates do not. What I have found is that the candidate often says something to the tune of "The others I have talked with have already answered all of my questions". If that's the case, then you asked the wrong people your questions. This is the hiring manager who is ultimately going to make the decision, so you better be asking them things like, "What criteria are you going to use in three months to evaluate and determine whether I'm exceeding your expectations?", or "sometimes I like to work double shifts to get ahead of things, is the office open 24x7?" Good questions.

Informing the boss

Yes! You got an offer! Note that I didn't say

you are expecting an offer- you got one. If you're just expecting an offer, then mum's the word to your boss and co-workers until you have truly landed the offer document.

You probably think informing the boss of your departure will be easy or fun. It might be. However, in most circumstances, you should approach informing your manager in such a way as to not rule out a potential counter-offer. You might be surprised by the sudden revelation your boss has on how much he depends on you, and the prospect of interviewing and trying to hire and train someone else is daunting. You need to give him the opportunity to have this revelation. If you go in guns blazing, that won't work.

Why do you want a counter offer? Why not? Having another option is always good. Changing jobs could be a hassle, so maybe if the counter offer was good enough, it would be easiest and best for your career to stay. Who knows? At least give yourself an opportunity to really find out. Maybe you have read somewhere and believe that you should never accept a counter offer? That, plain and simple, is BS. It's true that you should never accept a counter offer if you think the company is truly hosed or that the environment is so poisonous that you just can't stand it anymore. Duh. However, if they offer you a pretty penny more and/or a different title, you should seriously consider it.

In order to get approval to make a counter offer, your boss will have gone to a lot of trouble getting approvals, writing justifications, etc. If it makes sense, reward your boss. There is almost no stigma attached to somebody who accepts a counter offer anymore, and the places where there is a stigma won't offer you one anyway. On a personal note, I've accepted two counter offers while at the same company, and it has worked out very nicely for me.

Here's how you should approach telling the boss. First, don't tell anyone else outside of your family. If you tell co-workers or colleagues before talking to the boss, your chances of getting a counter offer just went to crap. No manager wants it widely known that if you go and find another job the company might give you that raise you deserved three years ago and keep you there.

You should certainly be completely happy with accepting your new position and plan on that being the actual course of action that takes place, when going in to inform your boss. You don't necessarily need a letter of resignation in hand. I would generally advise against it. You can always email or drop off the letter later. If/when you do write it, keep it super simple. "I have really enjoyed working at OldCompany and will miss the people tremendously, but I feel this is the best move for my career" works nicely.

When you tell your boss you are resigning for another opportunity, he/she may ask if there is anything they can do to keep you. Your answer should be along the lines of you had not really thought about that as an option, so you are not sure. You can then mention that the new position pays more and has the coveted "Senior" title, and that's the main reason you are leaving. If you say something like, "I really dislike the direction the company is going", or "I can't stand working with these nutjobs", you will not receive a counter offer. These are things that the boss doesn't have control over, and are things that he/she cannot change.

The boss does have the rudimentary ability to request more money or a title change for you, though, and that's what you should go for. In trying to determine how much money you should request, the offer at the new place should have nothing to do with it. The fact is, you need to determine how much money you would need to make you stay and be very happy with that decision. This should include a premium for having to work with the nutjobs and having to go along with the new direction of the company. It has nothing to do with the amount of your new offer. In fact, if you are asked what your new salary will be, the answer should be the amount that it will take for you to stay at the current place.

Finally, don't worry about the new company if you do end up accepting a counter-offer. You should very nicely inform them that you have had second thoughts and have decided to stay where you are currently. You could try and tell them that you have accepted a counter-offer in the hopes that they will make you an even better offer. That does sometimes happen. It's really up to you on that one. The main thing here is that you should have no remorse or bad feelings about accepting a counter offer. It happens all the time, and it's just business, my friend. The same way it's just business when the decision is made to outsource jobs or lay people off.

6 HANDLE THE BOSS

Dealing with the Bad Boss

Chances are you are going to have a realyl bad boss sometime in your career. I have seen it all. There are managers that are terrible at dealing with their team and play favorites. There are managers that are afraid to ask anything extra out of the people on their team, and let them walk all over them. Worst of all is the manager that doesn't recognize when they have a star employee. Since we are focusing on you becoming a star employee, we need to get out in front of this and take care of things so that you get the recognition, promotion, and salary increase you deserve.

I'm going to make a couple of assumptions for my first set of advice here. First, I'm going to assume that your manager is someone that can eventually be won over if you know enough about his/her goals and execute on the right things. Following that, I will assume the opposite, and that's where things can get very interesting.

Assuming we are just dealing with someone

you haven't been on the same wavelength with, that is readily fixable. First of all, following much of the advice presented thus far in this book may very well heal and expand your relationship with the boss. If not, then do the following:

1. Meet with your boss, find out exactly what he/she wants you to do.
2. Do it.
3. Do it faster and better than he/she expects.
4. Ask for more challenges.
5. Meet those challenges.
6. Repeat.

You do those things, and you are going to be on your boss's good side. Obviously, you can't go around with a chip on your shoulder or an attitude. If you're strutting around thinking that you are smarter than the boss (you likely are), or that you don't need that buffoon's input (you do), you will quickly convert your bad boss into a serious problem boss. We don't want that. Get over your attitude- we are going for a promotion here, not an ego trip. Always keep your mind on the end game.

Now, let's assume your boss is a complete idiot. He can't give direction, or when he does and you flawlessly execute on the direction, it turns out he wanted something else. This happens every time. Every damn time. There is no way to win. You're stuck. You are faced with what I call a real BOSS- "Big Old Stupid Shit". There are many BOSSes out there. In the private sector, in the government, and low and behold, right there managing you. What's one to do?

Let's start off with what not to do. Don't waste your time trying to change or understand the guy. We've already established that's not possible. Certainly don't get into arguments with him, that's going to make you look bad to anyone around, even when you are unquestionably right. Don't try and make your boss look bad to others either, that will occur on its own. Recall, the BOSS was put in charge of you by someone, and that someone might very well still be there. Your BOSS is probably telling his boss that many of the current problems are because of you. That bastard.

Well, you need to get out of there. Assuming you want to stay at the same company, you are going to need to find a new position with a new boss. This may be a lateral move, for the moment, as your key goal is to get to a manager that will appreciate and reward your star performance. How do you do that? Good question.

First, look around. Is there a manager that people always say good things about, or that exudes good vibes whenever you run into her in the hallway? Ask yourself, "Who do I want to work for in this place?" Then, get courageous and set up some time with that person, if they have an opening or not. Fifteen minutes is all you need- do it formally or informally. The next time you see her in the hallway, just say, "Hey, if you have 15 minutes some time, I would like to run a couple of things by you." If you already have a relationship where you feel comfortable setting up a 15 minute meeting with her, do so. Make the body of the meeting invite something like this:

Hi GoodPotentialBoss- just wanted to set up a few minutes with you to discuss future opportunities on your team. If this time doesn't work, I'm pretty flexible so just let me know what time would work.

Thanks,

FutureStarStuckUnderBOSS

Then, when you do meet, you need to keep a couple of things in mind. Your goal is not to get onto her team right at that moment. It's highly unlikely that there is just a spot sitting there that you can move into. You should bring a copy of your resume, preferably one that highlights the skills that you think will come in handy on her team. You should not put down your current BOSS, or disparage him in any way. He should be a non-factor in this discussion. Instead, focus on your career aspirations, and how you think moving to her team and working on projects there will enhance your skill-set.

At some point, she is going to have an opening on her team, and you want her thinking of you first for that position. Even better, you can almost be guaranteed that she will encounter the same thing that every boss in the technology field encounters- more work than what she has resources to complete. This gives you a couple of ins. The first in is that since she knows you want to work on projects in her area, she might just ask your BOSS if she can borrow you for a project. You definitely want that. Borrowing a resource can easily turn into a permanent situation.

Otherwise, you can also make the grand suggestion. You could suggest that if she has a project that needs additional resources, you are so eager to start working with the technologies, etc. that you are willing to put in 4-8 hours of your own time each week to help out. Nothing says "I'm serious" more than putting in your own precious time to work on something new. That's a pretty good start with the new boss too- she now knows you're the type of guy who doesn't fear actual work. I bet she has people on her team right now that fear getting work, and avoid it like the red monkey plague. Yep, you're looking good already.

You have won the day, now get out quick.

Good news! You are in that meeting, and you finally got whatever you were asking for. Hooray! You have a bunch of questions, though, and you start rattling them off. Bad move. Get your butt out of that meeting and celebrate. Now is not the time to ask for details, that's a classic rookie mistake.

I know this because I have certainly made that mistake. I can very distinctly remember the time when I did a beautiful presentation for my boss's boss when I worked at a large software development shop in the "Automotive Software Industry". Yes, that industry does exist.

I presented in stunning detail, a well-thought out plan on how to transform this fugly, unstable system that was causing our customers all kinds of problems. The solution detailed the systems that would need to change, and the resources required to make those changes. It highlighted the expected, magnificent outcome, which involved high customer satisfaction and potentially more revenue. Very nice.

To give credit where it's deserved, the boss's boss understood. He asked really good questions. He explored the other options, and brushed them aside and agreed with the one I had chosen as the right way to go. He was a decision-maker, and he said those magic words, "let's do it". I'm pretty sure I visibly smiled ear to ear, and maybe even gave a grunt of delight.

Then, something nasty snapped in my thick skull. There was an audible "squish" as a piece of my temporal lobe dropped right off my brain. I was going to have to execute on this plan. A plan the higher ups were now aware of and from which they expected great results. My instinct was to start retracting some of the strong statements that I had made in my presentation and to start asking questions. I began with, "Ok, how should I put in the requisitions for new headcount?" I followed that with, "How do I get the additional hardware needed?" I then rattled a bunch of other stuff off, until my boss had the good sense to usher me out the door. I had succeeded, yet I had failed.

That's a lesson learned, and one that you, hopefully, are able to learn the easy way. When you get what you want, get the hell out. Express your good-great gratitude, and then blow that joint. You can sort out the details in follow-up meetings or through email, or whatever. Take your reward and bask in it. It doesn't matter if it was like the situation I described above, or whether you just got the promotion. Ask the detailed questions later!

One-on-Ones

Many times, as a technologist, you will be subject to a reoccurring phenomenon known as the "one-on-one meeting" with your boss. This typically reoccurs either every other week or on a monthly basis. In the tomes of management philosophy, this type of meeting is thought of as an important thing. Personally, I hate calling it a "one-on-one", it just sounds a little seedy . One little known secret about this type of meeting, though, is that your boss dislikes it as much as you do.

When you notice this meeting on your calendar for tomorrow, you start to mentally prepare responses to questions about projects and the like. You have to come up with a list of things to talk about to try and fill that thirty minute void. Well, your boss is doing the same thing. She's hoping that you don't ask anything about compensation or a promotion. She's desperately hoping that you haven't been waiting for this meeting in order to deliver bad news about some project that you are working on, and she's definitely hoping you don't have anything to complain about that will generate more work for her.

What should you do?

Like anything else that's not pleasant, but mandatory, you have to find a way to get something out of it for yourself. Knowing that your boss doesn't enjoy these meetings will help you formulate exactly how to do that. One suggestion I have is to send her a status report ahead of time, hopefully showing how things are golden. You can then take the opportunity to discuss things with your boss that will make her life easier. Does she need you to take the lead on a new project? Does she want you to follow up with the support group on whether they are ready for the new functionality to be released? If you have anything negative to say, you should follow it up with the recommended solution, and you just need her go ahead to execute on it. Don't give her extra work. You want her to think of any meeting with you as a pleasant experience.

This is also a good forum to bring about your ideas on process change. You absolutely need to be thinking about processes and how small changes might bring about large benefits. Defining process change, as discussed earlier, is one of those things you need to be doing to make it to the next level. Bring her a flowchart of the current process, and bounce an idea off of her about a minor change that would be easy to implement. Ideally, the change will result in faster time to completion for projects, a higher quality output of some kind, or a happier customer.

What's that? You can't think of a process to change? Yes you can. Look at what you do every day. If you are a developer, I can guarantee that you could easily find things to do differently in the code review process (establish one if you don't have one), unit test writing process (start writing them if you're not), or the overall implementation/hand-off to QA process. If you are a QA person, I'm betting you can easily come up with process changes to interact with the developers better, make sure you have complete test case coverage, etc. If you are a support person, I know you can figure out a better way to log calls that come in and get the customer the help they need. If you are a DBA, I bet you could sure use some more process around documenting what the hell you are doing to the production database. Hopefully you get it. The business is always evolving, and technology is always evolving, so your processes need to evolve too. Be that person that comes up with changes.

Another way to come up with process changes is to simply look at the last five major issues that made it to your manager. Take some time and figure out what could change so at least one of those issues doesn't make it to her (that's a 20% reduction in escalations, my friend). Recommend that change at your next one-on-one. She will be thrilled, and you are on your way to a promotion. One word of caution, though. Don't recommend a change that will cost a lot of money or is too complex. "We need to get a CRM solution in here to replace our current system", is not going to work (even if that is the best solution). Recommending a process change that is not reasonable to implement is the equivalent of not doing anything. In fact, it's a bit worse, because no matter how satisfying it might feel, you gain zero benefit from being in the "I told you so" position. Avoid getting in that position, and instead be the person who can recommend and implement simple process changes that will make a real difference. Do it!

Your Assumptions are wrong, again

As a fully competent technologist, you will undoubtedly run into the situation where you have made a poor assumption. In the field of information technology, it's almost always the case that you have imperfect information and therefore will need to make some decisions without knowing every detail. The key for you to retain that "fully competent" rating is to not let your bad assumptions affect how you're thought of at work.

The best way to minimize the risk of an assumption turning evil is to take a step back every once in a while and ask yourself, "What could go wrong if I do this?". This is an especially useful technique if you are working on a project that is about to be released into the wild. You have done all of your development testing, things have passed QA, and they are ready to go into production, right? Maybe.

Start recalling all of the things that went wrong the last time you did something like this. Assume complete ignorance from the customer or from the other systems that your new software has to interact with. Tell your manager that you think you have thought of everything, but can she think of anything that could go wrong? I have a fairly extensive trove of bad assumption experiences, one of which I will relate here.

Interestingly, many of my bad experiences relate to release nights. In this case, I was a lead technical architect at a major computer maker, and about to release into the wild a brand new online payment method. The new payment method was basically a company branded credit card that a person could get approved for on the fly, and instantly use to complete their order. Pretty cool.

Development was a real struggle, as was QA, since part of the project involved interacting with a third-party that handled the actual execution of a credit check and delivering the terms and conditions of each user"'s individual account back to our system. We will refer to this third-party and their system as "dumb". In addition, this third-party was buffered by yet another team and system where we actually sent the transaction to. We will call this second third-party and system "dumber". I bet you smell a rat here. I wish I had.

When we finally had a QA environment up and running that could take a transaction end to end, we had to fix a lot of stuff, which made this ultra-important project late. Finally, though, we got everything working in QA. Neither I, nor my partners in crime, had made any contact with anyone who worked on system Dumb, which is the system that actually determined a customer's credit worthiness. We only interacted with those who worked on system Dumber, and they assured us all was ready to go on their side. My bad assumption was that I could trust Dumber to manage Dumb, and that they would know if all was truly A-OK.

Again, here we are at 1:00 am on a Tuesday, rolling out code. The good old release document had been successfully pared down to 20 pages, and I personally made sure the guys who rolled out the code had read it and understood all the steps. It was still kind of bumpy, as these things always are, but at about 2:00 am all had been rolled out. Then, all we needed was to run a couple of transactions through the new payment method, and then let all of our customers reap the rewards of paying with a super high-interest rate credit card! The smell of success was definitely wafting through the hot Texas early morning air.

At about 2:01 am, someone must have turned on a valve that spewed poison into that air. The first real customer transaction came back as "Could not complete-error". Company's Love showing those messages to customers. Attempt two yielded, "Error, transaction void". Naturally, these were two error messages that we had never seen returned before in QA or development testing. Fortunately, the Dumber team was sitting in the release war room with us. They immediately took charge and traced the error messages back all the way to the Dumb systems. One of them even had the phone number for the Dumb technical support center. Dumber put the phone on speaker and dialed away.

"Beep-do-Beep, the number you are trying to call is no longer in service. Beep-do-Beep". Nasty.

"Wait", said a Dumber team member, "I have the home number of the guy I always work with."

Back to the speakerphone we went, and sure enough, Dumb answered on ring 11. Dumb was pretty tired sounding, and was unaware that we were doing a major software release that integrated directly with his system. After he shook off his grogginess, his first question was a real doozy, and instantly became a cult classic at work.

"What the heck, are these transactions coming from the Internet?"

I still get a chuckle thinking about that, and a rustle of fear down my spine. You must recall, this Texas computer manufacturer I was employed at had made their name and billions of dollars by selling computers directly to consumers online.

The Dumber team was speechless, so I answered the question for him.

"Yes, indeed they are. However, you should

be receiving these transactions in the same format as you get any other transaction from any other system."

Dead silence for over a minute.

Finally, Dumb spoke up.

"Well, I can definitely tell you what the issue is. Our system goes into Sleep Mode from 12:00am to 8:00am eastern, and doesn't accept any transactions during that time."

Now it's years later, and I still tell people I'm in Sleep Mode when it fits the situation, even if they haven't heard the story.

There you have it. Bad assumptions, bad outcomes. Hopefully, you can use this example as your own, and you won't need to go through the learning experience directly yourself. You have to take a step back and ask yourself the difficult questions, and then get with the right people who can assure you of a correct answer.

7 BEING THE BOSS

You just started your new role. I say "role" because that is the very handy term that all management and HR types use when they don't want to call you by a specific title. Your new role is Senior Developer, or Lead, or Technical Manager, whatever, it doesn't really matter. It also doesn't matter if it's at a new company or at the existing old battleship. You are new to your role, and here is your chance to not screw up and also to begin the launch to the next even better role. That's right, you should already be thinking about what's next.

Technical Management Philosophy

When you become a manager, things can get pretty rough at times. No one appreciates the difficulties you have to deal with on a daily basis, including employee problems, project problems, and of course upper management problems. However, there are a few concepts you should always practice and you will find that being a manager is not only tolerable, but perhaps even rewarding. When you hear your employees say things like, "You're the best boss I have ever had", it hits you right in the tear duct. What's even more amazing, though, is if you can get your employees to say that *and* get your projects done ahead of time. Now, that's a real accomplishment.

Listening

Ninety percent of being a good manager is about becoming a good listener. Let's face it, you already know what you know. You aren't going to get any smarter by dominating conversations with your employees, and you're certainly not going to win them over that way. You need to listen, and let them finish with their spiel before starting in with your opinion or thoughts. If you are new to the management role, you probably think that if you let the employee speak their ideas first then you have to accept them. That is certainly not the case- first in doesn't win. You have the final say, so relax and listen to what they have to tell you.

A key to listening is availability. Make yourself available in all the normal formal ways, such as the lovely one-on-ones and other scheduled meetings. Also, make it clear that not only do you want to have people stop in and talk with you randomly, but that you reward such behavior. By reward, I mean the reward of getting time talking with the boss on any subject under the sun. People really, really appreciate that. You need to make sure that everyone on your team feels comfortable waltzing into your office and telling you about the amazing time they had at the Kenny Chesney concert last night. When you establish that kind of relationship with your employees, not only is it a great work environment, but it also provides a really good path for you to get projects executed. If your employees like you personally, when you ask them to do something professionally, they will do their best work. If you are a jerk-of-a-boss, what type of output do you think you are going to get?

Rule with Common Sense

As the manager, you get paid to make decisions. There will always be multiple different ways to do just about anything in IT, so you need to be definitive about your decisions and explain them thoroughly. Even if your team doesn't 100% agree with you, they need to respect your final decision and execute on it like it was their own. The best way to get that kind of response is to do the same thing with your employees- give them credit for good decisions they make, and respect their input into the decision.

When you have to make a tough call and you're not sure which way to go, the best thing you can do is to resort to common sense. Let's take a fairly typical example. The business wants a new piece of functionality, and there are a couple of different ways to implement it. Technique "A" would be considered the right way by the architect on your team, which involves a significant amount of code changes, testing, and risk. Technique "B" would be the "hack", which would get the business what they need in short order, but it wouldn't promote good programming practice and therefore is considered inferior. You have diligently listened to the options from the technical architect, and now you have to make the decision. What do you do?

You do the hack, of course. Why? Common sense dictates that the best thing for your team, you, and the business is to get this project done quickly. Even though the team may think you are weak for making that type of decision, in reality you are helping them out by establishing that you and your team understand the business need and want to deliver on it as soon as possible. Also, you can't ignore the fact that to most developers, architects, etc., pretty much anything that takes a short period of time gets classified as a "hack". As a technology manager, you need to be able to ascertain when something is a "negative hack", meaning it really will affect future scalability or maintainability, and when something is a "positive hack", meaning the developer or architect prefers some other method, but this will do just fine.

You should also establish a culture of common sense. There are typically two main types of opportunities to do this. The first is when you are explaining a decision to someone on your team. Take them through the details that led to the final decision, and then simply ask, "Does that make sense?" This allows them to see how you came up with the decision (sometimes with information they don't have, such as business need), and that you value a pragmatic view on things. By taking them through your reasoning, they get visibility into your decision making genius, and may even start to apply the same technique to their decision making.

The second type of opportunity is to reinforce the use of common sense whenever you can. The best way to do that is when someone on your team explains an idea to you, simply respond, "That makes sense." Again, you are reinforcing that making technical decisions is done primarily around logic versus emotion.

As a side note, I arrived at the whole common sense/makes sense approach while working as the VP of Software Development at a large organization. My teams developed and maintained commercial software in a very competitive market. For whatever reason, I always found myself replying to ideas or decisions that I agreed with by saying, "That makes sense." After about two years of doing this, I noted that almost everyone on my team and many people on other teams started using that very same phrase. I had accidentally created an environment of people that valued and analyzed ideas from the standpoint of whether the idea truly had merit or not. When I finally realized that people were following my lead by doing analysis on everyday items and by evaluating if it made sense or not, I felt truly pleased. More importantly, a lot more decisions were made based off of logic rather than preference. Preference will get you into a lot of trouble.

Time Off

Congratulations again, you're a manager! You get to make decisions on things like project direction, which resources to put on projects, and yes you even get to decide whether you are going to approve your staff's vacations or not. Here's a tip- always approve vacations. You don't need to be screwing around with people's private plans. You know you are going to need these people to put in extra effort at some point, and you need them to do it willingly. Declining vacation days is akin to saying, "Sorry, your work life is more important than anything else." That's simply not true.

As a manager, you are in the number one position of making your employees work lives either good or bad. Nothing matters more than an employee's direct manager in terms of whether they like working for a company or not. You are the most direct bodily representation of the company to your employees. Even if you can't stand your own manager or he's a number one jerk, don't funnel that down to the people you manage. You need to filter that garbage out, not pass it along. It is always a challenge to decide what information you should deliver to your employees, and which information you should filter out. My advice is, be a HEPA filter. Start by filtering everything, and then gradually start to inform your team with information that is clearly relevant or important. Never pass on your management's bad attitude, though. The fact is, you and your team can still be successful even when the company is not necessarily doing well. In fact, that's the absolute best time to be successful as upper management starts making decisions on where to cut costs.

When an employee informs you he or she is sick or has a death in the family, there is only one appropriate response. "I'm really sorry to hear that, take as much time as you need". You have no idea how powerful that one sentence is. You are telling your employee that you trust them, that you understand they have a health or personal issue, and that you completely support them. That's the kind of stuff that will be remembered about you long after you are gone. That attitude also gets vicariously assigned to the company, and over time it becomes a "great place to work". The last thing a person needs to worry about when having a health issue is work. You have their back on this, they can depend on you. That favor will be returned a million times over by quality of work and willingness to go to bat for you when you need it. However, that's really not quite as important as the fact that you, as a manager and representative of the company, are helping to make meaningful decisions about the quality of life that people lead.

Take Responsibility

Another key about being a good technical manager is you need to take responsibility for the things that go wrong. If someone on your team delivers a major defect into the production environment, that is your fault. To the outside world, you are the team. Don't offer up the head of someone on your team when an issue occurs. Issues always occur. That's why we technologists stay employed. Naturally, you cannot let major problems happen without talking with the individuals responsible for them and correcting things for the future. You need to get your point across and then decide whether you need to invoke a process change or make other improvements. Your team will appreciate you for this, and so will your management. Of course, when things do go well, you know that your management assigns the credit to you as well, so it only stands to reason that when they don't go so well you take the brunt of it.

Another thing to avoid: there will be times when you are in a one-on-one or other such meeting with an employee, and you end up willing to agree to anything just to get the person out the door. Don't do that. Don't tell your employee something that you don't intend to follow through on. This is called integrity. When you say you are going to do something, you need to do it. It's ok to reconsider a decision later, but you then need to directly inform the person that you have decided on a different course of action instead of what you discussed with them. It's also okay to just say that you need to think on the best course of action and that you will get back with them in the next couple of days. Then, of course, you need to get back to them in that timeframe. That's the way it works if you want to be a manager- you need to be as honest as possible and do what you say you are going to do. A lot of the other management stuff just comes naturally in line if you follow that simple principle.

On a similar note, it can be very tempting to use the "boss" excuse when telling your employees "no" to something. "I would approve your new computer request, but Bob will just reject it". That kind of response seems good because it puts you in the positive and your boss in the negative, and it's easy- really easy. Don't take the easy route.

The fact is, you are in charge. Do you think

the request for a new machine is valid? If so, you need to push through the request. If you don't think it is valid, then you need to state your reasons why. That takes courage. Being a good manager takes courage. Blaming it on the next level of management is simply not acceptable. It's only okay to do that on big issues where you have earnestly tried to get something through and it gets rejected. Then it really is your management's fault and not yours. Again, this is called integrity.

Motivation

Alright, now pay attention here because this is probably something you don't agree with. You, as a great manager wannabe, need to motivate your employees. Yep, it's part of your responsibilities.

I can hear you whining now-"People need to be self-motivated" or "They are getting paid to do their work, that's the motivation". Both of those statements are very true. However, don't you want your team to succeed and be better than all the rest of the rabble out there? If so, then you need to help them succeed by letting them know that you truly value and appreciate their work. And it doesn't take much to do that.

First and foremost, you must remember the previous points about keeping your office door open and being highly available to the walk-in. This goes a surprisingly long way to motivate people. Employees like being able to brag to others, "Yeah, I stopped in and spoke to Bossman and he said to go ahead and move that requirement to phase 2." This makes the employee feel good, keeps you in the loop on important decisions, and motivates people to do a good job.

You should also employ all the classical approaches to motivate people. Do they go out for coffee every day? Then surprise them and pay for it once in a while completely out of the blue. Out of your own pocket, too. People respect that much more than you using the company's credit card- it's more meaningful. Your job is to become a great boss because you want to be successful. Being regarded as a great person to work for leads to success for you and your team. It's really that simple.

Do the occasional outing- mini golf or museum or whatever. People remember and are motivated by that stuff. It shows that you actually care about your people as much as you care about your people's job results. That makes a real difference on how much your employees are engaged at work and how well they do the work. It also makes it a lot easier to have difficult conversations with the team when things don't go so well. They respect you and will listen to your constructive feedback. That's really all you can ask.

www.ingramcontent.com/pod-product-compliance
Lightning Source LLC
Chambersburg PA
CBHW071221050326
40689CB00011B/2402